I0377189

Witches, Women & Words

Also by Beatriz Copello

Women, Souls and Shadows, Bemac Publications, Sydney

Meditations at the Edge of a Dream, Glass House Books, Sydney

Under the Gums Long Shade, Bemac Publications, Sydney

Forbidden Steps Under the Wisteria, Abbott Bentley Pty Ltd, Sydney

A Call to the Stars (translated into the Chinese language), Crown Publishing Company Ltd, Taiwan

Beyond the Moons of August, University of Wollongong, Thesis Collections

Lo Irrevocable del Halcon, Bemac Publications

Beatriz Copello

Witches, Women and Words

Acknowledgements

Some of these poems have been previously published as follows:
'The Witches' Brew' and 'Spellbound by the Moon' in *Bluetongue Tasting Anthology*
'The Witches' Forest' in *Ambitious Friends Magazine*
'Maleficarum' and 'Defiance' in *Live Encounters* Volume 1
'The Winter Solstice' in *Clitlit Literary Journal*
'Obiter Dictum' in *Listen to the Inner Voice of World Peace*, Edizione Universum, Italy
'Refugee' in *Messages from the Embers*, Black Quill Press

Witches, Women and Words
ISBN 978 1 76109 287 9

Cover image: Seraphina Martin

First published 2022 by
GINNINDERRA PRESS
PO Box 3461 Port Adelaide 5015
www.ginninderrapress.com.au

Contents

Witches – an explanation

'Women are invoking the witch to find their power in a patriarchal society.' – Sofia Quaglia, *Quartz*, 1 November 2019

'When for "witches," we read "women", we gain a fuller comprehension of the cruelties inflicted by the church upon this portion of humanity.' – Matilda Joslyn Gage

'Pam Grossman, author and host of the popular *The Witch Wave* podcast, said witches are having a resurgence among feminist who want authority over their lives.' – in Mary E. Corey, OAH *Magazine of History*, Volume 17, Issue 4, July 2003, pages 51–59

'The witch is a feminine archetype who has authority over herself. She doesn't get power in relationship to other people. She has power on her own terms. And because of that she is,I believe, the ultimate feminist icon.' – Pam Grossman in an interview with Laura M. Holson, *The New York Times*, 11 October 2019

Witches

Surrender

I ride at low speed on my witch's broom
over houses and streets through open windows
there for all to see   despair   deceit   anger
husbands that cheat   abused women
girls fucked by their fathers.
alcohol   numb brain   loneliness and isolation
hunger pains   the lot of the poor.
abuse and abundance   by the rich and powerful.
empty of dreams   the unemployed,
drug addicts turned into muggers
the women of the night hope for a new day
politicians plan and plot   bankers count their loot
a grey mist envelops the city   pollution
a sharp turn I take and escape this world
once in my coven I throw away my broom.

The Witches' Brew

I throw in my cauldron
my first communion veil,
my prayer book and
my mother's wedding ring
soon I stir in two tears
one for her and one for me.
The dry flowers
from my wedding gown
I break into bits
to boil with the rest.
My history books
full of men's tales
and absent women
to the cauldron go.
For two minutes I boil,
with rosemary and rue
together with a pinch of anger,
a teaspoon of oppression,
and a nip of abuse.
The bubbles reflect
on their brilliant surfaces,
the portrait of the many
who tried to contort me.
I let the brew burn dry
until the moon announces
the birth of a new woman
a woman who is free.

Genesis

Words
scrambled
in the mind
puzzles
conundrum
confusion
and then
a force
touches them.
Magic wand
artistic spell
and the words
are strung
one after the other
like beads
in a necklace.
Out of chaos
creation –
a poem born,
the poet
a god.

The Mystic Wand

When she was born the witches
congregated to plan her future,
with a mystic wand they drew
on a smooth and radiant stone.
She will be free and powerful,
her chores she will decide.
The goddess Aranhod
will protect and bless her
and she will speak her mind,
others would respect
and admire her brain.
On a stormy night an evil warlock
named *Patriarchy* turned the stone
to sand. Without the plan
then woman became a cart
that travelled through a road
paved by men and the church.
Time went by, no magic tricks
women carved their paths
a new beginning a redrawn plan
sand will be turned back into stone.

The Witches' Forest

Hymns of past glories,
holding hands
the witches sing.
In the sacred fire
their offerings burn.
Ritual of love
to save the forest.
A malignant force
from beyond
the abyss of Apsu
is axing down the trees.
Gaia mother hear
their prayers of pain.
The verdict is final
the 'Greens' have lost.
The witches invoke your power
to change the forest fate.
Remember they chant
the perfumed gums
the moon reflected
on the glowing leaves,
the birds singing
in the mornings
and your sacred soil
turning into sap.
The witches' bridal chamber
will become a coffin
save the trees mother Gaia.

The Angelus Call While the Witches Dance

Hear the Angelus bell
it is time for prayer!
There they go
to the revengeful god.
The picks, the tools, the pots
all are set to rest.
The able walks to church,
the sick will pray at home.
Millenary dogma
that enslaves the innocent,
sorrowful procession
that bow to peremptory laws.
Repent sinner!
Flagellate your flesh,
pay now your dues.
Plaster statues
dressed in silk
and fake jewels.
Candles and incense
burn for your salvation.
Beware. He sees it all.
He watches, he judges,
He points his finger at you.

Weathered faces,
furtive looks,
hands that tremble
fingering rosary beads.
Lips, fast moving in prayers
prayers to the almighty
who never forgets.
Gullible devouts,
run, escape,
open your eyes,
come to the forests
where the witches sing.
Their prayers are sung
under the moon and trees.
Crowns of rosemary
and lavender flowers
the witches wear,
and they dance at midnight
while Mother Earth
embraces each and every one.

Maleficarum

They called them 'witches'
and they died by fire
sometimes hanged
others by drowning
innocent women
healers and midwives
who lived on their own
they were wise females
independent and self-sufficient
reveres of nature and Earth
the populace perceived them
as evil and imagined them
huddled over a cauldron
to create potions and poisons
boiling bones and frogs
the 'Hammer of Witches' dictated
how to identify the sinners
who cohabited with the devil
torture confession death penalty
demonology at its zenith
persecution of those
believed to be heretics
sorceresses' power
their knowledge to cure
to console suffering
to bring life into the world.

Spellbound by the Moon

Spellbound by your magic
I have crossed an abyss.
Your alabaster skin
is my mandala
and your mysterious eyes
conjure me to love you.
Mystic feelings
dreaming in the nights
bathed by your light.
Your image is my icon
your rays my healer.

Prayer to the Witch of All Witches

I have a wish to make
wave your magic wand
venerated mother
witch of all witches,
invoke your powers
and bless this world.
I want the children
to breathe clean air
and drink pure
and crystal water.
Restore the sacred land
so crops will grow again.
Reduce to dust
those mountains
of plastic and trash
and don't forget
to blow away
the acid rain.
Cover the ozone hole
and cure the cancer
of our suffering skins.
...and please Mother
help women
ascend to power
to prevent
more damage and pain.

In the Winter Solstice

Ritual of love
in the winter solstice
delectable fragrance
of the burned offerings
myrrh and myrtle.
Supernatural strength
from our healing powers.
Circle of witches
around the sacred fire,
oracles and incantations
with crystals in our hands,
we speak in women's tongue
while the tree of knowledge
cast playful shadows
on our purple gowns.

Obiter Dictum

she sat at the end of a dream
holding in her hands the stem
of a plastic flower
solemn
sad
simple
trajectory of an angel
blinded by fury
encounter of the souls
who don't ask permission

to live
to beg
to adore…

the ones who hold the power
the ones who control
the ones who dominate

conquer
the conqueror
they do
determine the length
of the life of the poor
the pauper
the unemployed
the sick
plants die without water

the miserable shed tears
mothers cry
and politicians give speeches

solace

sublime

silence of the dead

do they have hope?

Defiance

A universe hidden in your palm
power ingrained in your cells
Who are you blaming destroyer?
Ignorant of our fears you immolate
the innocent as well as the rebel.
Universal joke your power
to create miracles. Blessings
to the hens who lay eggs
and the roosters who sing
when the sun rises in the horizon.
Predictability of protons, neutrons
or light travelling through empty space.
Like an oyster living in a hard shell
shamelessly you hid our inheritance
in one of the pockets of your robe.

Escape

Time knotted at her throat
like a silk scarf worn in autumn.
Pulled away from reality
in dreams she becomes
a winged being who travels
she extends her hands to touch
the faraway, the impossible.
In this space that is only hers
time does not exist
pain is only the fantasy
of a madman who believes in God
where the light is subtle
where no accusers thrive
and guilt doesn't touch her
she is no longer a prisoner.

Inferno

Ignorance that castigate this land
priorities determined by a few
the ones who wait for Argamedon
the ones who allow the hollowing of Earth
those powerful who adore non-existent beings
the ones who sell our water, our ports, the coal.

Bare land, empty of life, black forests
burnt trunks like innocent bystanders
see the days pass, skeletons of trees
naked branches – arms to the sky
waiting for rain and the return of life.

Carcasses on the side of the road
Burnt fur, rigor mortis, eyes closed
a crow pecks the carcass
hunger and thirst of those who survived
I drive only the road is in front of me.

Religion

No rights in Inquisition
cantatas and pogroms
humanity debased
moral quicksand
beings shaped
by unscientific scalpel
all seeing gods
of unfounded superiority
with pedantic philosophies
imagined powers
of the supernatural kind
surveillance and enforcement
must discharge obligations
to the spirit world
trick at hand
eternal damnation
a price to pay
a prayer or a blessing
money making adventure
archaic ruling defunct

Humans

Depression

Without suspicion she lets it through
creeps in and sinks to the pit of her stomach
covers her like a black and thick cloud
numbs her senses, her feelings, her whole being.

She observes life pass by like in a deep tunnel.
as an innocent bystander she negotiates events
inert and mute she hates living and like
froth on the top of a wave she dissolves.

Life painted in grey: sips sorrow
Life opaque and absent: swallows tears
Life devalued and worthless: drowns in self-pity
Life dull and desolate: plans her death.

One day departs…

Somnolent and rigid she crawls out of her cocoon
dizzy and vulnerable she confronts life
scared she learns to walk again
step by step
now she lets her blood run wild.

Even After

Perpendicular dawn of a waiting game
death…not far away…ever present,
solitude announces itself like a cat in heat
while the persistent southerly
is a foreigner on this piece of soil
where his bones will turn to ashes,
a blue mist hides the mountains
…and now it is night dressed
in her black and silver dress,
acrid mouth, an absence
that overtakes the moon
which is a child's scribble on cardboard.

God

stones in her mouth
frozen in a corner
like a rat chased by a cat
a prisoner her mind
rules, dos and don't dos
repressed anger encased in cellophane
he stands there rigid like a monolith
sharp face finger pointing
as he commands and admonishes
she disintegrates, her edges melt
leaving her body, she no longer hears him
where is the young woman? It is dark
a sombre room, no door, no windows
suddenly he thumps the table
startled the escapee returns
'Yes,' she mutters.

Hope

Blind walking through a perilous life,
senses dormant like a tree in winter.
Desolated forests of dead branches
which snap under heavy steps.
Hidden under the fallen leaves
and the decaying humus
feelings of regret, entangled mass
of roots, deep seated in his beginnings.
Poison ivy growing on trunks
sucking   sap   sap   sap
a heart in debt – guilt guilt guilt.
The so called cruel, the one who is dead,
he sees   he sees   he sees
the perennial sassafras
envelopes him with
the subtle perfume
of its bark which bewitches him,
the one who despairs he who believes
he is a gypsy moth – *Lymantria dispar*
to live is a challenge, hope is slender
like fairy grass, delicate like maiden hair
and he makes a commitment. He chooses life.

Inheritance

Ancestral anguish printed in our cells
patterns of behaviours that lead the way,
our eternal mothers' dreams travel through time.
Encoded messages flow through our veins
patterns copied into cells. Preferences...
Likes and dislikes are these our decisions?
Is the scroll of life written in the past.

Mortuus Est

He wants to hear that voice
that tells him what to write
the tongue in his mind is mute
words have frozen
like a blade of grass
he prays to the god inside
the one who has jailed his stanzas
and anchored his lines
in the river of his imagination
no phrases surface
to the edge of his consciousness
meaning lost...purpose obscured
like the inside of his shoes
he makes hopeless attempts
to create to give form
to his hidden feelings
the blank screen flickers
wait wait wait
for his fingers to type
has his brain overdosed
on symbolisms, metaphors
imagery, satire and similes?
has the critic inside killed the poet?
no answer, no poems, no sonnets

My Friend the Poet

Shadows creeping slowly
obscuring lonely window
light at speedy pace escapes
through drawn curtains.
A light bulb hangs
from the ceiling
on a black cord
covered in flies.
In the middle of the room
a single bed, centrepiece
of a pauper poet
and a wheelchair,
witness of pain sits in a corner.
Scattered on the floor
Books, newspapers, clothes.
No computer or iPad…
Poems written on sheets of paper
make a blanket on his limp body.
The carer found him dead
holding a pen on his hand.

Our Essence

I am you and I am I.
I follow life gamely
like an impertinent,
pretentious shadow.
The divine dust in me
is your ancient dust as
it is my blood, my cells, and
the perpetual essence in me.
… And your pain is mine
like it is the space
that separates and joins us
because there are no distances
between souls, only in
atoms – colliding particles
of neutrons and protons,
life eternal…
death a metamorphosis.
… And again I am
the lion that eats the deer
and I am the deer.
I fly above flapping wings
with flamingos in formation
creating a red cloud.
I am a Japanese fighting fish
hidden in aquatic forest
waiting for its prey.

I am a Balinese dancer
chased by ghosts and devils
my feet floating above
evergreen rice paddies
in the theatre of existence.
A king, a poet,
a teacher, a dreamer,
a lonely beggar,
an orphan, a tyrant,
I am all until death
sneakily reaches me again,
then I become perfume,
a rock, a star, a dream
...a dream dreamt by someone
dreamed somewhere
in this infinite universe.

Refugee

(Australian fires)

She saw the smoke turned black
it was like a childhood nightmare
tentacles that reached her
arms that chocked and strangled
and then the fires sprouted
like wild mushrooms here, there
and everywhere, soon these became
violent flames which devoured
the undergrowth and climbed
the old gum trees like agile athletes
in seconds the canopies were alight
the unbearable noise resonated
like thunder in her ears and
her heart was an engine at full speed
she grabbed the suitcase which contained
the history of her life: letters, poems,
documents and photos and ran
she sped towards her car and
turned around for one last look
but instead closed her eyes
once safe in the car she asked herself:
Where now?   Where now?

Reflexions on a Dead Man

I

As in a scene from Dante
where fire and heat
consume all passions
a man has entered
a place for lost souls
where the dead rest
till judgement day.

II

Truth   covered
by a white linen sheet.
Truth of the stigmata
on a man put to rest.
Undeniable truth,
of a now silent sinner.
Truth about the price,
paid for the life he wore,
like a silk handkerchief,
in the right pocket
of his tailored suit.

III

The witch in the cauldron boils
a pinch of pain, two tears and
the shadow of a man.
Dyeing the widows weeds
she stirs with a spoon
the black liquid
that holds,
her love.

IV

Do the dead feel cold?
Do they suffer?
Does hunger rumble in their bellies?
Do the dead want to live?

V

Pages that kept a secret
between the pages of a book
like a Brazilian butterfly
kept to dry after her death
the secrets flattened
pressed, and muted

VI

Autumn
perhaps the season
of the ageing souls
perhaps the season
when passions sleep
autumn

She Told Me

(Australian fires)

I saved my children,
and my dogs and the budgie
but I lost my chooks,
and my precious horses.
My husband is angry
he doesn't speak to me
because I chose to leave
and not to fight the fire.
I have no house, no shed,
my past is dead, as my garden is,
it went up in flames, only
the ashes of my photos remain.
My children want their toys
the baby wants his blankie
and wonder why their father
doesn't play with them.
I can't sleep and cry
at nothing. We live
all in one room at the back
of my sister's place
'Get rid of the dogs,
and the children are noisy,'
she screams every day.
I tell myself all will be fine,
as it always was, but a voice
inside me whispers,
'There are wounds that never heal.'

To Neruda

To have been your *Araucana*
to have been your muse
to have been the sea
embracing your abode
and when awake
find your tenderness
or see you
calmly sleeping
after our ardour.

To have been
your postman
the wine at your table
the glass that your hand held.

Your eternal words
were leaves amidst a storm
yet they carried fire
steel and hope.

But you have given me
the company of your poems
the gift of your wisdom
the belief in your ideals.

Wisteria

Purple shawl that covered
the patio in spring
its tangled branches
responded to nature's
urgent mandate,
and bunches of
perfumed buds
one by one opened.
A solitary child
sat under the wisteria
dreaming of better times,
a child who learnt
that marriage alone
does not keep
parents together.
The wisteria heard
the child's prayers
making promises
to an omnipotent god
who never heard
the begging wishes.
When summer came
and the flowers died
the wisteria dressed itself
with its best green.
Would her parents
stay together?
She wondered
eyes to heaven.

Then as time passed
one by one
the brilliant leaves
turned to gold
and like miniature kites
descended onto the patio.
The bare branches,
which twisted and winded
on the metal frame
told the child
it was autumn…
The house was sold,
the suitcases packed
not only with clothes
but also with the memory
of the wisteria in flower.

Yet Not Despair

She walks the tightrope
a balancing act, eyes closed
uncertain future awaits
no net, no outstretched arms
to catch her

yet no despair…

Now she is a boat
a small rowing canoe
struggling against the current
the waves furiously bounce
against the flimsy nutshell
she is about to capsize

yet no despair…

Paper mountains encase her
she is in a cave, in a dungeon
about to be hanged

yet no despair…

Her inner strength shines
in her intense black eyes
always love in her words
as her world collapses.

Peccator

Piping hot
five hundred in his pocket
velvet jacket
dry whisky taste
she cries in a corner
ice nightmare
one more man for the day.
Dice roll
glued eyes
tomorrow perhaps…
stone gurgling water
terrors and errors
'Please enter.'
Fun inside

The Social Order or Disorder?

Fantasy

Ephemeral fantasy,
glory and ecstasy
perdurable chimera.
Reason or lies?
She hides, amongst
those who are blind.
She walks, head high
even though
her future has vanished
behind clouds of envy and
controlled anger.
Everyone has forgotten
how to say 'sorry'.
She is now the moon
disguised as a lake,
then a tree, a fruit,
a leaf, a seed
mothered by the soil,
fertile and loving.
She has said everything,
words have frozen
on her lips and her hands
in prayer, mock the mad
who beg for reason.

Generate Event

A key measure
promote anger
petulant leader
hands busy twitting
critical situations
demands made
control systems set
obliterate and humiliate
bits of data
stored and guarded
no signs of hope
apocalypse of biodiversity
Salamandrivoran triumph
circuit board
buttons to press
countdown on…
overload of words
Hoopoe headwear
challenge overruled
causality encompasses
choice engine
predictable behaviour.

En Garde

Horizon behind dark clouds
bleary loneliness empty vessel
runs no longer – time has stopped
waiting for a dream
like waiting for Godot.
The invader lurches
and attaches itself
like fungus to a rock
sits there spreading
its poisonous tentacles.
The needle has been threaded
ready to embroider
silver stars on a shawl
when night finally arrived
it caught me unprepared.

Quarter Pounder

The faulty china dolls,
baked from dust and a spark of sapient
reign in a decaying world.

A brook sings a monotonous song
obscure chanting of pebbles rattling and
at the bottom – fool's gold waiting.
A trail of dreams all the way to heaven
a maiden weave with nylon threads
a giant net to catch an eagle.

Soldiers march blindfolded and mute
to defend a future of heat and floods.
The streets are deserted, at the dinner table
families sit to a meal of images
imprisoned in a wooden box.

The powerful play chess with nature
ticks bursting with blood,
fungus growing with lust.

Earthly concern: war, guns,
cars and planes, gadgets, trips,
MacDonald's, and the pill
to stop the ageing process.

Humans joined by plastic,
rubbish, and the need to consume,
while the mind of all minds
cries at the failure
of the china dolls.

The Prophets

Words produced without meaning
phrases aligned because they were demanded
crude sounds vague answers…
Do all fears stem from an intuitive knowledge?
Unbalanced equilibrium, culpable reason
to see the fire burn of a differential criterion
validity created by people who fall into the power trap.
Can we recognise ourselves in those
who govern and create the rules?
Hope is hidden like a miser hides his riches.
The paupers count crumbs and the homeless
steal corners under a blanket.
And those who blindly fornicate the present
continue consulting the oracle…
yet the truth is there for all to see.

Up North

Red ochre, vibrant soil
which like notes penetrate
not only the eyes but the soul.
Vast land that swallows water
where anthills appear to be
silent penitents in prayer.
Here and there pink flowers
break the monotony. Sad.
Sad lament of crows in flight,
they descend onto their meal –
a dead kangaroo victim
of speeding drivers or perhaps thirst.
No chisel-sculpted rocks
which during dawn metamorphose
into scaring beings to chase
defilers of sacred places.
Dreamland of dreams to be
where gums dress in many forms
and the earth bewitches us.

Solitude of waterholes
Which like a caring mother
gives of herself and sustains
the ebullient and vibrant life
that flourishes under the sky,
a cloudless blue, bright blue,
silk blue sky…and then
slowly grey shapes opaque
nature's colourful narrative.
How many thousands years
has this silver-studded shawl
covered this bejewelled land?

Winter

Ancient souls
sharing old dreams
yellow pages
in this calendar
of lives long lived…
Steps on the road
of this peaceful dawn
petals of dry flowers
flowers which once
were fresh
as our hopes.
Tired bones
lucid minds
leaving memories
which when forgotten
piece by piece
will disintegrate
into the infinite.

'a' For Affray

abject destiny of an intense love
abrupt departure of kindness
abandon cursory sentiments
abase your arrogance and
abstain from hate and nastiness.
absurd behaviour of a once
affectionate and kind soul
anthology of excuses
abide without apologies
abysmal thoughts
absolution not given to
acerbic words and
artifices.

it is easier to beg

subtle incongruences
mysteries unsolved
corrupted feelings
pain and solace
two rivers flowing
in opposite directions.
encounters   disappointments
a heap of illusions
rocks tumble down
who asked for a piece of life?

Nikola Tesla

Slowly he enters
into a world of sombre shadows
where cadavers rest without concerns in a life parody

scared of them
he wants to pray but how?
Anchored to his shoes there is one metal ball

one note sounds…
on a one-string discarded violin
a deaf man cries as he meticulously plays Chopin

a dog barks
the closed eyes open to see
what or who is waiting behind the closed door

pain pleasure sex
memories hidden in a sick mind
rancour disguised as love flagellation in the initiation
ceremony

salacious mind orgasms
a stick that writes on sand
inventions plus madness, poverty and loneliness

he wakes up
the nightmare left like his pigeons
but what is left? Electricity energy and the magic numbers
369.

Weed

Lawbreaker in search of novel emotions
fire and smoke to the lips   fingers tremble
the heart palpitates and expectation arises
a search in a dense forest   mind divided into boxes
overcrowded like fans at a soccer match
wait   think   what now   forgotten habit
memories surface   laughs   hunger
neurons that produced Dopamine
expectation 20 minutes wait
it arrives   now serotonin oxytocin
and endorphins combine
a burst of happiness envelops the body
music is heard note by note
colours are brighter   life allures

but now…what the hell nothing
just a calling from 'the sack'
hopes for a good night's sleep

Sydney Siege

Flowers on the ground
a message of humanity
in this crazy world.

Drowning sorrows
in a box of chocolate
I cried watching TV.

A gunman brought pain
but also awaken in us
acceptance and pride.

Aleppo

Fires burn
charred flesh
blood flows
silence no longer
run…but where?
Dead yet alive
stomachs rumble
dry of tears
they tread lightly
on poisoned land
stench and sorrow
the unburied rot
the alive wait
waiting for what?
No doors to knock
no ears to hear
the innocents' cry.

www.ingramcontent.com/pod-product-compliance
Lightning Source LLC
Chambersburg PA
CBHW062158100526
44589CB00014B/1867
* 9 7 8 1 7 6 1 0 9 2 8 7 9 *